Dedication

This book is dedicated to my Momma, Linda Kost. You have always believed in me even when I didn't believe in myself. Through good and bad, you have stood by me, holding my hand, and encouraging me. I would not be the person I am without having an amazing mother like you. Life hasn't always been easy, but you are an inspiration. I can only hope to be half the woman and mother you are. I Love You!!!

For anyone who has faced the storm, fallen down and found the strength to get up and fight again, may these words help and inspire you.

Contents

Acknowledgements

I am not even sure where to begin thanking those who have been with me on this crazy journey. Writing was a dream I never even knew I had. However, I know this is the path I am meant to be on in my life. Words can heal and inspire. Reading them can be your voice when you have lost the ability to speak. I hope mine will help those in need and inspire others.

First and foremost, I want to thank my Momma, my rock, my anchor and my truest friend in this life. Without you, I would be nothing. Saying thank you and I love you does not seem to be enough for all you have done and given me, but I will spend the rest of my days saying those words, so you know without a doubt how sincerely I mean them.

To my beautiful daughter, Shelby, you are my heart and soul. God sent me an angel the day you were born. Your determination in everything you seek in your life inspires me. No matter what has been thrown at you, you never quit. I am beyond proud of you! I am honored to be your Momma and cannot wait to see what and where life takes you. Remember Baby Bee, the sky is the limit; never stop reaching for the stars. You deserve each and every one of them. I love you so much it makes my heart hurt!

To my husband, maybe I should apologize to you for having to put up with me? I know I AM NOT the easiest person to live with, but after all these years, the ups and downs, you deserve a medal for not choking me. Thank you!

To my family, Gramma Shuss, Jen, Vernon, Jeanette, John, Michael, Mary, and Ed thank you for your love and support. My life would be so boring without you. (Ha ha) They say you can't pick your family, but I would pick you and am thankful you are mine.

Clara Fox and Layla Stevens, sistas from another mista, saying thank you is not sufficient enough to cover all the love and support you have given me. You never let me quit and never turned your back when the going gets tough. You both are a piece of my life's puzzle, a piece of my heart, and I cannot imagine my life without you. No matter where we go, no matter what we do, I know we will be on this journey together. I cannot wait to see what comes next! I love you both immensely!

T.H. Snyder, Angel Steel, Wendi Hulsey, Isobelle Cate, Amanda Lanclos, Julie Morgan, and Nicky Jayne, thank you for taking a chance on a newbie. I am honored to be part of each of your books. It was a pleasure writing for you and I look forward to reading whatever you dream up to write next.

To the Webb family, Nicole and Robert, thank you for allowing me the honor of writing a poem to capture the beauty of your love story. Robert, I pray you get the heart you need. Nicole, I love you girl!

To Joshua Brown, thank you for the honor of writing a poem for your beautiful Mom, Lori. It is moments like this that make writing worth every second.

Gena H., Bill S., Diane W., Nink E., Skye L., Pam B., Levi H., Crystal B., Natalie L., Melissa A., Heather F., Sherry N., Rachel W., Jim L., Dina R., Linda W., Shelly J., Kathy B., Wendy H-J., and Martina Z., you are the most wonderful friends a girl could ever ask for. Your support and love me unconditionally. Whether we talk every day or whether life pulls us in a thousand directions, it just seems like yesterday that we were together or talked. In light or dark you are always there supporting me and encouraging me. I am so thankful to have you in my life. I thank you and love you!

To D.H.H., thank you for opening my eyes and making me realize I was so much more than I was allowing myself to be.

Taya Hardenbrook, TH Designs and Eric Battershell, Eric Battershell Photography/FITography, thank you so much for taking my vision and making a gorgeous cover.

Rebecca Cartee, with Editing by Rebecca, thank you for the fresh set of eyes.

Casey Harvell, with Fancy Pants Book Formatting, thank you for making my book look so amazing!!! I can't tell you how much I appreciate all the help you have given me to make this all happen.

To the readers, THANK YOU for buying my book and supporting me. Without you where would any of us authors be?

My Words

The words that flow
Are sometimes slow
To stop the hurt
I hold inside
I let them go
For all to see
In hopes I am not alone
In this sometimes harsh and cruel world

The games we play
Webs we weave
People we become
Aren't always because
Of choices we made
Rather from the pain caused by another

Words are like knives
They cut deep inside
Leaving you to bleed
Even if they can be forgiven
They will never be forgotten
Some haunt you for the rest of your days

But little by little
With the start of each day
You are given the chance
To try and fight again
To see the sun
Breathe in the fresh air
Be thankful for all the little things
That truly make life worth living for

Every person that steps onto
The path you are walking on through life
Has a reason or lesson to teach you
Be open to it all
Don't close your eyes

No matter the lesson
The choices is always yours
To fight for yourself
Or let the ignorance of another win
Come on now think
You are worth so much more!

I reach out my hand
In hopes that another
Will take a hold and learn
From my mistakes
Or celebrate in my successes
If my words can do this
Even for just one
Then I am rich beyond my wildest dreams

Can I

Can I forget the hurt
Let go of the past
Start over again
Be just friends
After all we've been through
Can I

I can't lie
A part of my heart
Will always be yours
What we shared
Was more than some ever will
But I see through your lies
I am not the broken girl you left behind

You played the game well
Took more than you gave
Shattered my heart to pieces
Without even saying an
I'm sorry
Not even a goodbye
You left
And never looked back

I laid down
I gave up
It took me a long time
But I got up
Dried my eyes
And started moving on

I always wished you the best
I wanted you to be happy
To have the life and love
You so desperately seek
You deserve that
So do I

You cannot make someone feel
What they don't feel inside
No matter how hard you try
It will always be a lie
They will always seek more
No matter how many times
They come knocking at your door

Can I let go
Can I move on
Can I forget
Can I forgive
Can I be your friend
I can, but it will always be
 Way more
Then you deserve

Days End

The day is done
It's time to unwind
Let all the stress and worries
Float along
Like the water over the rocks
Of a babbling creek

Close your eyes
Breathe deeply, relax
Focus on all the good today held
Even the smallest of goals
Are achievements
Remember only you can allow another to hurt you
And only you can hold that hurt inside

Release all thoughts
Into the brook
Wave goodbye
Free yourself from any hurts and burdens
Lesson learned
It is time to unwind

Tomorrow is a new day
Put one foot in front of the other
Set new goals
What can you achieve?
Even if it is just making another smile
What a success you have achieved
Sweet dreams
Sleep tight
May the angels and spirits guide you
Keep you safe and warm
Heal your body, mind, and spirit

Greet tomorrow with open arms
And a smile upon your face

Faces

The many faces that I wear
The daughter, sister, mother, wife, and friend
The role I play
Is different each day
Constantly changing
To fit what someone else
Needs me to be

Sometimes I forget
Just who it is
That I really am
Who I am meant to be
While playing the other roles so diligently

Time goes by
Days into weeks
Months into years
One after another
Until one day you wake up
And wonder
Who am I?
What do I like?
What are my interests?

The kids are gone
Everyone is busy living their lives
The nest is empty
No more blaring radios
House full of friends
It is time to decide
How you will find
That person you can now be

The sky is the limit
No one to hold you back
Take that trip
Sign up for a class
Write a book
Find out who you are
Now that the years have passed

The faces may change
As the years go by
All of those faces
Made you who you are today
Take what those roles have taught you
And start living your own life again

Gone

Hold me tight
I need you
I am calling for you
I cannot find you
Why can't you hear me
I feel so empty

Why would you leave
How could you just leave me
Wasn't I worth the fight

I gave you my all
The best of me
I wanted it all
Couldn't you see

You took my hand
And raised me up
Told me to be proud
Stand up tall
Forever you said
Surely was not long enough
Even an eternity could not cover it all

To be with me
To love me
And experience everything
We wanted and needed

But you left
Left me alone
To face it all
Alone and cold
You don't hear my cries
Won't take my calls
You said I love you
And then you were gone

I Gave My All

The bitter pain of a jilted heart
That gives all it can
Time after time
And gets back none

Always seeing the gray
In between the black and white
Always forgiving
Begging for more
A heart full and loving
Now shattered to pieces

I gave and gave
But all I had to give
Was not enough
You wanted more
Demanded and took

Your words were lies
Empty and meaningless
Your heart black
Deceitful and cold
Your intentions
Malice and manipulative

You built me up
To tear me down
You promised forever
And then left me to wonder

What did I do?
What did I say?
What can I do?
I would take it all back
Beg you to stay
Change myself
Whatever it takes

You hurt me to the core
Took pleasure in my pain
Left me at rock bottom
Then came crawling back
Pleading your case
Promising to change

The truth of it is
I am too good for you
And even promising to change
Things will never be the same

All the shattered pieces
No matter how you try
Can never be put back together the same way again
The flaws and holes will always show through

You used my inner demons
Played them against me
Pushed me until I cracked
Abused me until I broke
My eyes are open wide
I can see the light of day
No longer will these eyes cry for you
I have come a long way

Julie Mühler

I Knew

I knew the moment
Your eyes caught mine
Forever would not be long enough
To spend with you

I knew when your hand reached out to hold mine
Our fingers would fit perfectly together
Like pieces of a puzzle

I knew when your mere touch
Sent electric shocks through me
The connection between you and me
Was rare
A special treasure
A blessing from above

I knew when you asked me to dance
This would be the first of many times
I would melt into your strong arms
The melody of a song background noise
To the true music I heard
When I laid my head on your chest
And your heartbeat played my favorite song

I knew this was the night
All my dreams would come true
My prince charming
My knight in shining armor
My soul mate
Has finally found me

I knew as the days and weeks went by
The love we shared was one of a kind
And when you dropped to your knee
With tears in your eyes
Asking me to share your life for all eternity
My heart soared

I knew you would come to me
I saw you in my dreams
I will never let you go
No amount of time
Would be enough
My heart and soul
Are yours to keep

I knew from the first look
I knew from the first touch
I knew
I knew
I knew it was you

I Remember When

I laid awake
Night after night
Praying to God
You would come back into my life
Stared up at the stars
Wishing you would text me
Tell me you were sorry
I was the one
I held your heart

Time went on
The hurt slowly went away
I stopped making those wishes
Quit praying to God

My heart was numb
It was better off
Than feeling the hurt and rejection of
What you did
Over and over again

You played with the heart
Of a broken, weak girl

Showed her love, happiness, and fairytales
You promised forever
A whole new world
But those words were empty
Told to every girl

You walked away
Without a care
Took it all
Never looked back
You did not care
What happened all those months
While you were gone
The tears that were shed
The hopelessness
The despair

Now you are back
After all this time
Saying hi
Wondering how I am
Like long lost friends
That share no past
I am not that girl
The one you left
I found myself
Through all the hurt
You may have taken me for a fool back then
But never again

You had your chance
You chose wrong
I hope you enjoy the view
Of me soaring high
Seizing the opportunities
That have been put in front of me

I am sorry
You could not see that in me then
I hope someday you sit saying
I remember when

Julie Mishler

I Thought

I thought about you today
I think about you every day
I wonder how you are
What you have been up to
I know I shouldn't
I try not to

Reality is you were a player
You played a good game
But the fantasy behind it all
Was like a dream
I never wanted to wake up from

I see your face
When I close my eye
I hear your voice
Saying my name
It all takes me back
To a time
When I thought you, me, and forever
Was truly going to be

I still want the dream
I am sure I always will
I saw a new life
Full of possibilities
Full of love and happiness with you

How do you just let that all go
Time may fade the vibrant memories
But even time cannot erase
What I feel inside my heart

In My Arms

Calm your mind
Rest your eyes
Lay your worries in my hands
For just a little while
Put your head on my chest
Listen to the beat of my heart
Trust in me
I will keep you safe

The angels will spread their wings around us
Heal our bodies and minds
Rejuvenate our souls
Bring peace into our hearts
As we close our eyes and put an end to another day

Tomorrow is another chance
To start again
To let go of the past
And step into today
With our heads held high
Smiling for all to see

Good morning beautiful
A new day has come
Breathe in the fresh air
The sun is shining bright
Make today your day

The world is a better place
With the beauty of your face
And kindness of your heart
Share it with the world
It is rare indeed

I will always be beside you
My hand out reached for you to hold
To face whatever may come our way

The team of you and me
Can never be defeated
We are strong as individuals
Stronger united as one

My love for you will never fail
Safe in my arms
The world stands still
Hearts beat as one
Time stops
I will protect you always beautiful girl

Look

"Look in the mirror"
You command me to do
Demanding me to see
What it is in me
That you see

"Look past the obvious"
It is deeper than that
Those deep blue eyes
Have so much to say
They are the windows
To your soul
Where your true beauty lies

It is not in your pant size
It is not in flaws
Those flaws make you
Beautifully you
They tell the story of your life
Of good and bad
Happy and sad
Of the person you are today

You are so much more
Than you allow yourself to be
Holding back because of fears
But those fears
Are you judging yourself
Not what others really see

Will there be some superficial people
Yes, that is inevitable
People like that have no place in your life
Hold your head up high
Walk away from them
They are holding you back
Weighing you down
You are in control of you
No one else has the power to hurt you
Unless you let them

Words are merely words
It is how you react to them
If you take ignorance of others to heart
It will eat at you until there is nothing left
The worst words said
Are the ones you repeatedly tell yourself
And convince yourself that they are true

Free yourself of any and all negative
No more!
There are so many people
Who want to see you shine
Who see your beauty
Who want to see you be happy
To flourish and thrive

Loving Bee

There are moments in this life
When you know without a doubt
That the love you feel in your heart
Could never be greater

But as time goes on
Days become weeks
Months turn into years
So many moments happen
And with each
You instantly think
My heart is again
Overflowing with love

My little Bee
These words are for you
I have loved you
From your very first heartbeat
Each time I see your beautiful face
I am reminded of all the memories
You have given me
The moments I thought
My heart was beyond full

No matter where you go
No matter what you do
I will be with you always
My love is like an old, worn coat
Wrapped around you keeping you
Comfy and safe
Protecting and guiding you
I will always be with you
For you see, my Bee
I am in your heart

I will love you
My precious little girl
Until my heart stops beating
And even then
I will love you
Until we meet again

You are the truest
Love of my life
My greatest accomplishment
Loving you
Makes my heart whole

Lover's Embrace

Candlelight shadows dance
Over naked silhouettes
On a cool spring evening
The breeze blowing the curtains
The scent of the recent rain shower filling the air
While soft music plays

Red silky hair
Cascades down onto
Sun kissed skin
He reaches his hand up
To tuck the ribbons of hair behind her ears
Fully seeing her beautiful face
As she lowers her lips to his

Bodies intertwine
He caresses her satin skin
With his strong, rough hands
Hands that are calloused
From the rigors of work
Day in and day out
Making a life for her
The woman he loves

As the music plays on
The candles burn down
The heat of two becoming one
Passion unfolding
The scent of love fills the air
Whispered words of admiration
Promises of undying love

Laying in each other's arms
Falling fast asleep
The priceless gift they have given one another
Another memory
Another moment
Where two hearts became one
Two bodies joined in love
And hope for another day
To be together
For infinity

My love for you will always be
Stronger than the ocean waves
Crashing onto the shore
I will love you
Longer than the endless seas

My love for you will never fade
I searched my whole life
To find a love like yours
No one will ever compare to you
You are my fairytale
All my dreams come true

Our bond is so rare and special
Many in this life will never find another
Who is their infinity
Where I end
You begin
A perfect circle of love and life

Our hearts fit together perfectly
Like a puzzle piece
My heart is yours
You are my soul

You held the key that unlocked my happiness
You will always be
The reason my heart beats
The reason a smile is upon my face
The best days I have had are because of you
And when I lay my head down each night
I know that I have been blessed
Blessed to be loved by you in this life

No matter where the road leads
Whether it is long and cold,
Dark and rainy,
Sunny and peaceful
I will always be with you
In your heart, mind, and soul
My love for you will always be

No Longer Me

The ties that bind
That made me blind
Played with my mind
No longer inhibit me

The reflection in the mirror
Is of someone I once knew
Smiling and laughing
Eyes brightly shinning

The darkness that crept in
Like a virus
Has taken its course
And I can breathe again
Hold my head up with pride
Accept who I am
Flaws and all

Perfect, I will never be
But imperfectly perfect
Yes
That is me

Love me or hate me
I will no longer hide
I will step outside
Breathe in the fresh air
Feel the heat on my skin
Put one foot in front of the other
And thrive again

Will it be easy
Definitely not
Each day is a new day
To try, try again
As long as there is breath in me
I shall never give up

Not A Day

Not a day goes by
When something doesn't stop me
From what I am doing
And I think about you

I look at the clock
And remember how
We used to talk
Throughout the work day
Waiting for each other
To begin and end each day

The setting sun
With its beautiful colors reminds me
How we wanted to share an eternity
Of sunrises and sunsets together
Hand in hand

I stare at the moon and stars
And think about all the dreams
We shared with each other
You were my sun
I was your moon
And all the stars were ours
To share with each other

Not a day goes by
That I don't miss you
More than you could possibly imagine
Forgetting you
Forgetting us
Will never happen

How could I ever forget
The other half of my heart
My soul mate
My best friend
My missing puzzle piece

Not a day goes by
I don't wonder
How you are
If you are happy
I will always wish you the very best
You deserve all the stars in the sky

You taught me so much about myself
You brought out the best in me
You taught me to never give up
To fight for me
And the person I want to be

Not a day goes by
I don't wish
I had one more chance
To talk to you
To hear your voice
See your face
And stare into your beautiful blue eyes

Not a day goes by
I don't think back
To the special times we shared
Even the hurt of goodbye
Will never change the memories
Of the love I felt for you
Because not a day goes by
That I don't still love you

Julie Mishler

One More Chance

For one more chance
Would you?

Give up everything
To hear his voice
To see his face
What would you give?

For one more chance
To change it all
To fix the wrongs
Make things right
Could you forget the past
All the pain he caused?

For one more chance
Would you risk it all
To hear his laugh
See his smile
Can time heal
All that has been broken?

For one more chance
Would you sacrifice
To kiss his lips
And whisper his name
To feel his body
Would it still feel the same?

For one more chance
What would you do
If you only knew
Things would change

He would be
The man he said he was
The man you fell in love with
The man you have missed and longed for
The man who held all your dreams
In the palm of his hand

For one more chance
What would you give?

Snakes Reign

My heart once broken
Now locked away
The key buried deep

A heart that once was
A blooming,
Flourishing heart
Full of love and joy
Is now dying and decayed

The walls came down
You crept your way in
Slithering like a snake
Coiling and hissing
Blinding me with your venom
Choking me with your tail
Crushing me slowly
With each lie you did tell

I was easy prey
Your fangs punctured deep
I willingly let you kill me
Slowly day by day

The bloody wounds
Healed over time
The scars reminders
Of the damage you left behind
My shattered heart
Slowly healed
Now fully guarded
Tight walls built around it

You may sneak
Continue to slither
But eventually
The axe will fall
Cutting off your head
And stopping your reign

The Dance of Love

I crave your touch
The way you run your fingers through my hair
Your lips on my neck
Pulling me closer
Igniting my passions

The heat of your body
Against my bare skin
The mere touch of your hand
Makes my temperature rise

I feel your desire
Your burning need
As your body molds into mine
Like perfect puzzle pieces

The growl of passion
As I run my hand up your thigh
Gently dragging my nails
Across your hip
Up your chest
And into your hair
Pulling you in for a deep, long kiss

The fireplace blazing
As we lay on this bear skin rug
Our shadows dancing on the wall
To the rhythm of our love
As the music plays on
The shadows now still
The fire burned down to hot smoldering coals

Lying in your arms
My head upon your chest
Your fingers lightly cascading up and down my back
You whisper words of love
As I drift off to sleep
I could spend forever in your arms
Dancing to the music of us

The Fear Inside

My hands are shaking
My heart is pounding
My mind is racing
My eyes are full of tears
I cannot breathe
My chest aches
The fear inside
Is capturing me

I fear the unknown
It rules my life
Stops me from shining
Ends all attempts at trying
Shatters any dreams
Leaving me feeling so hopeless

I want to fly
I really do
I want to be happy
Succeed and flourish
But the fear inside
Says NO!
Will I be judged

Or am I the one judging myself?
Why can't I ever say the right things,
Do the right things,
Just be myself?
Why can't I just let go
Of this fear inside?

When did life
Become so scary?
When did the simple things,
Like saying "Hi"
Take such effort?
Who stole my essence
And how do I get it back?

Once upon a time,
I was so much more than you see
Young and carefree
Full of life
And endless dreams
I reached for the stars
And tried grabbing them all
Not this shell full of fear
Who cannot trust
And hides behind excuses
Letting the fear win

Breathe, just breathe
You can do this
Face the fear
And take the first step
Take back my life
Chase all of those dreams
No more excuses
Grab the hands that have been
Trying to help you all a long

Tell the fear inside
GOODBYE!
I WON!

Julie Mishler

The Little Things

The little things
So small
Yet big
So simple
Yet hard
Have no value
Yet are so often forgotten

The little things
Cannot be bought
They are given freely from the heart

The mere touch is priceless
A million dollars could not buy it
The unspoken words of a hug
Could melt even the iciest of hearts
Letting you know you are never alone

Simplistic words of praise and encouragement
Have more value than any gift you can buy
I love you
Thank you
I am proud of you
Easy right?
More often than not left unsaid

Life flies by in the blink of an eye
Unlike a tree that grows for hundreds of years
Our time is limited

The little things
Are those we sit and wonder
Why we didn't say them
Why we didn't do them

If you knew today was your last
All those little things
Are the things you would cry and beg for
More time
To say the words
Give the hugs
Smile the smiles

Take time to remember
All the little things
And never let them pass by

The Old Oak Tree

Meet me by the old oak tree
As the leaves are changing shades
And the winds begin to chill

Wrap me in your embrace
Intertwine your fingers with mine
Let's run through the corn fields
Laughing as the days turn into nights

When the moon rises
And stars light up the night sky
We will build a fire
And listen to the music of the night

Katydids and fireflies
Sing the song of our love
The fire blazes bright
Such a beautiful night

Heat pouring from your body
Your lust filled eyes meet mine
Your hand on my cheek
Lips sweetly kissing mine

I love you for all you are
All you do
All you will become
The memories we have made
Can never be replaced
Every day with you is an adventure
A trip I am more than willing to take

As days turn to weeks
Weeks into years
We will always meet here
Under this old oak tree
A constant reminder of our love
Where two become one

One hand
One heart
One love
Forever
Rooted deep in the ground
Like that old oak tree

As Love I Seek

There is a love I so desperately seek
I will never stop searching for it
To find the other half of my heart
The half that makes my soul sing
My missing puzzle piece

There will be one
That begins where I end
And dreams the same dreams
Who can envision what I see
Who understands my insanity
Yet grounds me and keeps me sane

I want the companionship of a best friend
The protector of a father
The intense passion of a lover
A soul mate
For life

I don't seek material things
Someone to grow old with
Enjoy the days and nights with
A hand to hold until the end
When we temporarily say until we meet again

No road is easy
Of this I am sure
But knowing you are right beside me
Fighting the fight
I promise you
I will never give up
On you, me, or us

When I find him
I will simply ask
Will you
Walk with me through this life
Share with me all you have to give
Hand me your heart

If you say yes
I vow to you
I will protect your heart for an eternity
Even that won't be long enough
To be with you

My promise to you
Is to love you
Honor you
Be a 50/50 partner
On this journey of our life

I knew one day
I would find you
My life is now complete
Take my hand my love
And let's take our first steps
Of our beautiful life

Julie Mühler

Forever As One

Moon shinning bright
On a clear and starry night
As we lay on a blanket
Out back in the field
Watching the stars
Twinkling little lights
Shadows cast all around us
Music of the night filling our ears
While we held each other tight

The chill of the breeze
Against our hot bodies
Pulls us closer together
Your lips meet mine
In a passionate kiss
Your hands roam my body
Pulling me in deeper
As our tongues intertwine

Want becomes need
As the passion becomes heated
The longing to be one
Can no longer wait
I need to be with you in every way

Our bodies move as one
Unbridled passion
That seeks satisfaction
The sun rises on a brand new day
As I lay in your arms
Completely sated
I know for sure
This music is heaven

I would give everything I had
To spend each and every day
For the rest of my life
In your arms
Our bodies as one
Starting and ending each day
Together
Making love
Forever

Goodbye

In the dead of the night
A faint thumping drum
Through the silence of the night
Such a hollow sound
As rain pours down
Life stands still
Everything stops

A sullen figure
Head hung down
Fallen to its knees
Rain soaked paper
With ink smudged words
Laying on the ground

Cries of agony
Heartache and pain
Pierces through the stillness
Cutting like a knife
Screaming out why,
Why did you
Say goodbye?

The lifeless body
With the breaking heart
Tears streaming down her face
Never got the chance
To say a word
The choice was made

Months gone by
The coldness of his words ringing true
He left her with nothing
But a goodbye

Rambling through the days
Crying out at night
The unbearable pain
Keeps her awake wondering
Where he is
And most importantly why he left

Trying to move on
As hard as it is
To live life again
Faking her smile
It is just so hard
When he is always on her mind

Maybe that glimmer of hope she holds
Will bring him back
Her mind says yes
Her heart leaps in joy
Deep down in her gut
The truth prevails
He is never coming back
He said goodbye

Someone new has crossed the path
The rain ceases to fall
Sun shines through the darkness
Up off her knees
She stands tall

The remnants of his letter
Float off into the breeze
The hollow thump of her broken heart
Now beats like a strong drum

Hand in hand
They say goodbye
To the deep dark figure
That was once lost
In goodbye

Julie Mishler

I Must Go

My heart I wear
Upon my sleeve
My love is unconditional and forever
So you see

You knew when you came calling
I would answer you back
Open my arms
Welcome you in

Time had passed
But the fact remained
I love you now
Like I loved you then
I'm sorry I can't only be
Just your friend

Life isn't always
Black or white
There is an area of grey
Grey is where hope lives
Wishes are made
Prayers are prayed
Second chances are given

No matter how many times
I take you back
You are never going to change
You will always play the game
Of take, take, take
And I will give my all
It is the only way I know how

I tried to separate my heart
But that just isn't me
I deserve more than the games that you play
I have no choice
As hard as it is for me
I must turn and walk away

Forever I will love you
In my heart you will always stay
For my sanity
I must do this
Don't ask me to stay

I will walk away knowing
I gave it my best
It helps ease my mind that
You are happy and loved

Maybe someday you will open your eyes
See the err of your ways
Want to apologize
When that day comes
Don't pick up the phone
The bridge has been burned
Don't try building it again

Julie Mishler

Lady Moon

Clear dark night
Stars shining bright
The moon beckons me
To look up to the sky
Searching my soul
For the answers
To all that ails me

Lady of the moon
Hear my plea
Heal my heart
Mend my soul
Grant me the happiness
I so long for

Give me eyes to see
What is most important
A heart that loves
With no walls or burdens
Free my spirit
No more negativity
Let me soar
Take this doubt
No longer will it hold me back

If I must walk alone
So be it
I will accept the loneliness
And hope another
Finds the goodness in me
To share this journey

To walk along beside me
Take my hand
Fight for me
As a lover and friend
To love me unconditionally

For me
Just me
Nothing more
Nothing less

Nothing

I feel nothing
No joy
No sorrow
Just emptiness
Lonely in a crowded room
Too numb to feel

My heart once full
Now broken
I hear words of praise
Encouragement and compliments
But they fall onto ears that are deaf
A mind that cannot process such words
I feel nothing

For one who wears
Her heart upon her sleeve
Believes in romance
Loves weddings
Repeatedly watches chick flicks
It is as if part of me has died
I feel nothing

I remember a time
When my heart was bursting with joy
My smile never left my face
I welcomed each day with open arms
These days I am too tired to care
I feel nothing

I want so much
To feel again
For my heart to beat joyfully
The smile to be a permanent fixture upon my face
To hear my laughter once more
And never again utter the words
I feel nothing

On A Fall Night

The night has come
The work day is over
It is time to leave

I walk outside
As the wind picks up
Blowing across my face
I close my eyes and see your face
Feel the faint kisses
You once laid upon my cheeks

Remembering all the times
We stood under the stars
Watching the moon
Staring at the stars
Dancing to the sound of the music of the night

Rustling leaves on a chilly fall night
Your arms around me
Holding me tight

You took my hand
And kissed it gently
While leading me to the house
Back to our room

The fireplace was crackling
The candles were lit
Music playing softly
As you asked me to dance

Safe in your arms
I relished in your scent
Following your lead
Entranced by your words of love

The winds changed direction
As I open my eyes
The memory has faded
The moon is shining bright
Nature's music still playing
Its tantalizing song

But you are not there
You said goodbye
I am all alone
On yet another chilly night

The ache of my heart
Reminds me it was real
The dance
The stars
The moon above
Take me back to a time
When love was all we needed

Secret Place

Way back in the woods
Secluded and dark
Where the brook babbles
Sun streams down
Through big, old overbearing trees
Is my special place

A place where nature calms all that is wrong
I stop, close my eyes, and take it all in
The sights
The sounds
The smells
The tranquility and peace
Bring a sense of calm over my mind and body

On bended knees
I place my hand in the water
The current runs through my fingers
Like the sands of time
Wild and free
Never stopping
Without end
Where it goes
No one knows

The rocks and logs
Only deter the waters path
Like life's journey
You may stumble and fall
But you must forge on
Follow the current
Ride the waves
See where it may lead

You cannot lay there and die
You have to get up and push on
Follow the flow
Get back on the path
And see where it takes you
From beginning to end

The Masked Man

In the shadows
We meet
On a dark, dim night
You have masked your face
But your eyes tell all
The words of your soul

You burn with passion
Fire raging inside
Your body is aching
Craving for more
I am drawn to you
Your scent intoxicates me

The door slowly opens
And before me you stand
The lust in your eyes
Such a powerful man

You whisper your intentions
Who am I to deny
Your wish is my command
I am at your mercy dear man

I am defenseless to your touch
I melt into you
Your kiss leaves my breathless
On my knees I wait for you
As the dawn of the day
Lets the rays of light in
I find myself alone in this room

I touch my lips
And smile at how my body aches
Memories of the unbridled night
Of passion we shared
The feel of your hands, lips, and body all over me

I long for you sweet man
I hungrily await your arrival
Any way I can have you
I will take
No matter how long
I will wait

The mysterious man in the mask
That haunts my dreams
Calling to my body
Making me weak
I will find you again
In the shadows of the night

The Path

The path I walk
Is not all pretty
The stones do not all shine
Some lights have burned out
The trees are not perfect
They are worn and bent

I have ridden the waves
Of nasty storms
Crashed and burned
Laid down in the dirt
Stopped building
And let the fire
Burn it all down

Life is not all easy
No one ever said
It would be
But every second
Is worth fighting for
Each step a new journey

Do not live in fear
The tress will protect you
Spread your wings and fly
Fight the fight
Open your eyes
See everything life has to offer
Laugh often and love hard
Never forget the
Flowers, leaves, bees, and pebbles
That helped make the path
You walk on today

The past helped build the path
Your present adds more stones
The beauty surrounding it all
Are the people that have joined you
On your way

People come
People go
People stay

Cherish them all
For what they add to your journey
Thank them for the stones they left along the way

Light new lights
Shine the stones if you can
Fill your path full of beauty
By surrounding it with
Positive, loving, and good people

You are ready to soar
To take that leap
Take a deep breath
Reach out for the branches
Trying to show you the way
No more looking back
Get up
It is time to walk on the path

Julie Mühler

The Pit of Despair

Sometimes you wonder why
Why you even try
When all you want is to
Just break down and cry

You sit there
And ideally stare
Mind racing
Unable to focus
All the hurts you hold
Resurface
Inner demons attack
Is it karma
Or just bad luck

The dam breaks
Tears flow freely down your cheeks
Your chest aches
It hurts to even breathe
No consolation will help
The pit of despair
You have dropped down into

So tired of trying
And fighting to figure
Everything out
Taking on the world
Just to fail once more

Nothing is easy
Nothing seems to work
No silver lining
Anywhere to be found
Just mistake after mistake
Lined up
Glaring at you
Taunting you

Everyone around you
Needing and wanting
More from you
Pulling you here
Pulling you there
Expecting things of you
When you have nothing more to give

The tears slowly dry
The ache just dull
Demons repressed
Temporary stitches bind the wounds
Just too tired to even care

You made it through again
Fought the fight
Stood up from the pit
Dried your eyes

Now you wonder
As you sit and stare
Regaining your focus
This is not the end
It is the beginning
Of healing

Julie Mishler

The Tear

My heart is racing
Gripped with emotion
Aching in pain
My head exploding
With so many thoughts
The unanswered questions
The wondering

The pressure is building
I am trying to hold it in
Stay positive
You can do this
You have to fight
Don't think back
Live in the present
What is done is done

Never expect
Expectations are bad
The chains around my heart
Keep pulling tighter
The pressure has exceeded its maximum

The tears flow freely
Yet again I cry
For the love that is gone
The dreams now shattered
The unanswered wishes
And hopes floating through the dead air

Flow freely tears
Wash away the pain
Cleanse my wounds
Help me find my way again
Renew my hope
Dry my eyes
Help me hold on
Through this long, sad night

The Walls

You see this wall
Perfectly built
Brick by brick
Arranged by size

You stare and wonder
Why each one is different
And how they all fit
Like a perfect puzzle

Well let me tell you how
These bricks of all different shapes and sizes
Are the pains and hurts
I have endured throughout my life
Some are repeat offenders
Maybe I should personalize each one

People who have come
People who have gone
Broken promises
Empty words
Using my heart like a revolving door

Loves lost
Loves gained
I would rather be numb
Then feel the pain of another heart ache

Life moves on
Time waits for no one
The things we allow
The paths we choose
Are ultimately reflections of decisions
We have made

Little by little
Day by day
The bricks fall into place
Surrounding the heart
Protecting it fiercely

Maybe one day
A door will form
Allowing in one that is true
Until then the bricks are sealed
And this wall around my heart
Will continue to remain

There Was A Time

There was a time
Not long ago
When your text
Started my day
In a beautiful way
Throughout the day
Seeing your name come up on my phone
Made me smile so big
Knowing you were thinking about me too

There was a time
Seems like yesterday
When you were mine
Dreams were big
Possibilities were endless
I had a glow about me
The glow of happiness
Everyone could see

There was a time
I would give anything to have back
When I felt so loved
So special
My heart was full
I was happy
The future was so bright
I knew where I was meant to be

There was a time
I cried for hours
When you said goodbye
My heart shattered
I was so lost
You were my best friend
My love
You were my sun
Starting each day
I was your moon
Ending each night

There was a time
Not so long ago
When I awoke to a new day
The sun was shining bright
And even though the pieces of my heart
Are not tightly glued back together
I know somehow at the end of each day
The moon will rise
Stars will sparkle
Someday I will find that love again

Time

No amount of time
Will ever truly heal
A broken heart
Or change the fact
That you will always
No matter how long
Deeply care
For that person

The heart will always feel
Even when the mind
Knows the truth
Accepts the lies
Revels in the loss
Of the wishes, hopes, and dreams you had

Time may fade
Some of the memories
Time may take away
The hurt and ache inside
Time may pass
Where every second
Isn't spent thinking of them

A simple message
Can unravel
All the progress you have made
Because no matter how you try
How you lie to yourself
Or even to others
You waited for this moment
Prayed that they would come back

In that moment
When the numbness you
Masked around your heart
Unveils its cover
Letting you feel again
Your heart beats once again
Without those restraints
You will be reminded
Deep down it will never change
The truth

No amount of time
Will ever truly heal
A broken heart
But time will tell the heart
When to leave the door shut

To Say Goodbye

I wished for nothing more
Than for you to be happy
Even if that happiness
Did not include me
As I lay here
With tears in my eyes
I know the right thing is
To say goodbye

You found your way
Battled your demons
Followed your dreams
While I am still lost
Searching for the path
Needing direction
Looking for a hand to hold
But you are not here
You never will be
I am standing alone

I will love you always
I need to stop
Trying to be a part of your life
Let go of the idea of you and me
We will never be
Not even as friends
Your life is better off
Without me
I will never be
The woman you want
Live the life you live
I will always expect more
Than you are willing to give
I want your heart
Something you cannot give

I am so proud of the things
You have achieved
You have come so far
I know this is just the start
You will have all
You set out to have
You deserve that
And so much more

I will always remember
The time that we shared
I will never regret it
For it taught me a great deal
Opened my eyes
Made me see
There is a life out there waiting for me

I will find my way
I promise you this
Some night
When you are standing alone
Outside in the dark of night
Look up to the sky
The star you see
Shining bright
Is me
I found my way

Julie Mishler

When We Meet

When our eyes first meet
From across the room
The bond that we have built
Will be solidified
The connection of mind and body
Will answer all the questions
Squash any doubts
That love truly knows no distance
It transcends time and space

Your smile matches mine
My heart races
As I walk towards you
Into your embrace
Breathing in your heavenly scent
You place your hand gently upon my face
And give me the kiss
I have dreamed of a million times

I have waited for what seems like forever
To be in your arms
Here in this moment
I know with a hundred percent certainty
All the trials and tribulations
Lead me to this place
Where I belong

Your hand reaches for mine
As our fingers intertwine
A shock wave runs through my body
I shiver from within
Raising your hands to my lips
They fit together so perfectly
I close my eyes
Press my lips to your hand
And pray it never leaves mine

My heart once shattered
Damaged and flawed
Beats stronger now
The love you have shown me
Healed the wounds
Glued together the pieces
Even though the scars remain
They pale in comparison
To the new beat of my heart

Where I'll Always Be

Dear friend
Where have you gone
It has been so long
I have missed you so much
I am overjoyed to see you again

My love for you
Will never end
Our connection is so strong
Whether it be days, weeks, or even months
It is like we were never apart

You awaken the animal in me
Make all my senses thrive
The beauty of your words
The caress of your hand
I am dying to taste your sensuous lips
Feel your strong arms wrapped around me

Every time with you
Is an adventure
Of love and lust
Passion and overwhelming desire
You drive me wild
We connect so deeply
On various levels

You know my body so well
No words need to be spoken
I know we will never be
More than what we are
Right at this moment
But in that moment
That priceless moment
I am yours
You are mine
The memories we are making
Will be the happiest
I will ever have

I will cherish you
And this time we shared
If I never see you again
I will always have tonight

My dear friend
You will always have a piece of my heart
If you ever stop and look back
You will always know
Right where I will be

I have spent so long living in the past
Holding on to hurts
Relishing in the pain
Unable to move forward
To forgive and move on
The darkness finally overcame me
I laid down and gave up

I could not listen to those
Reaching out
Trying to pull me up
Showing me the way
I did not want to hear or see it
Rather, I could not hear
Through deaf ears and blind eyes

Any step forward
Turned into ten backwards
A good day was a present
A rare occurrence indeed
Faking it was my new name

Today though
Today, I saw some light in the dark
An epiphany if you must

That if I let myself soar
Take a leap
See what everyone else sees in me
Then maybe, just maybe
All the wounds that have been gaping and bleeding
Will slowly start to close

Like a butterfly emerging from its cocoon
It is time to shed the past
Stand on my own two feet again
Take a deep breath
Spread my new beautiful wings
And fly

That does not mean
The hurts are erased
Or that my heart and soul are healed
They may never be the same
But now looking back
Is a way to see how far
I have come
The lessons I have learned

Some inner demons will never rest
The beauty within falters
The doubts eat at your heart and mind
Those are the days when everything just hurts
And guess what?

It is okay!
Every day is a new day to try again
The key
The most important thing
You need to tell yourself
Over and over again
Never give up
Stand back up
Spread those wings
And take off in flight again

Julie Mishler

Without You

Silence consumes me
As I lay here in the dark
In the bed we once shared
Every little sound is magnified
Every creek and whine
The wind and rain makes
Whipping and hitting each window
Of the home you and I made

My arms are empty
I wrap them around my pillow
To try and feel warmth
Remembering cold nights like tonight
After the days end
When it was our time
Just you and me

Your head upon my chest
Caressing your hair
Hearing you breathe
Falling to sleep
Knowing you are safe
Surrounded by my love

My days are so long
Since God called you home
Never did I
Imagine living this life without you

You were so much more
Than I ever gave you credit for
If I could have one more day
Just one
I would tell you all the little things
I always should have said

I love you
You are beautiful
Thank you for the wonderful life
You made for me
For us
And especially thank you for loving me

The dawn is upon me
I made it through another night without you
I still feel you here
Your spirit rings through this house
I would give my last breath to have you back
God has no idea the angel He has

Please wait for me
When my time comes
I will run to you
And forever have you in my arms

Wolf

Remember all those times
We talked day to night
Wishing time would stop
So we did not have to say goodnight
The hours in between seemed like days
You were my sun
I was your moon
The stars were all the promises we shared
I prayed each wish would come true
And discover all that is hiding in your eyes

I think about your words
So loving and sincere
How could I have been so wrong
Why couldn't I see you were the wolf
Waiting to pounce on my heart

A heart so full of love and happiness
I thought I found the one
It was not just your looks
You mesmerized me from the start
You stole my heart
Even now my heart is in your hands

How do I unlove you
How do I forget
My world revolved around you
I was at your mercy
I saw a new life through your eyes
Every dream
Every wish
A lifetime full of love

I miss your smile
I miss your voice
I miss how you raised me up
But most of all
I miss the man
I thought you were
Even though in the bitter end
You were just a wolf
Dressed in sheep's clothing

You Deserve More

Foolish heart
So easily deceived
All that was healed
Now ripped apart
Gaping open
To bleed again

Simple words
From an ignorant man
Blind eyes and deaf ears
Will never see or hear the truth
To you he is perfect

He will never change
His rude, cold words tell all
Yet you blame yourself
Put yourself down
When it is he
Who failed you
Again

He is the coward
Playing with emotions
Being hurtful with words
Common decency eludes him
Why do you excuse it

One day he will see
What it is he lost
In you
In all of the relationships
He has that have failed
And no one is left
To fall for his games

One day you will open your eyes
See that you were always good enough
Forgive yourself
Trust again
Let the wounds heal

Smile
Because you deserve so much more
Than a man who
Holds you down
From shining like a beautiful star

You

Your smile
Lights up a room
Draws people in
Making them want to know more
About you
My heart so full
As I look at you with pride
And makes me want to smile with you

Your laugh
Full of happiness and spark
Makes others happy
Absorbing your positivity
Is music to my ears
A song I will never tire of hearing

Your eyes
Speak volumes
Of stories untold
Secrets locked tight
Of love and loss
Trials and tribulations
I could look into them forever

My life's goal
Will always be
To see your smile
Hear your laughter
And discover all that's hiding in your eyes

Your smile
My addiction
Your laugh
My heart's beat
Your eyes
My soul's savior

You,
You are my pride
My joy in life
You are my happiness
My saving grace
Loving you makes my life complete

Cry For Help

I call on thee
To come to me
Hold me tight
Heal my heart
Bring peace to my
Body, mind, and soul
Wrap me in your comfort

I am falling fast
Without a net
Reach for me
Pull me back
Into your arms
Back to safety

Night time is the worst
The world stands still
Silence is deafening
I close my eyes
Trying to fight back the tears
I have fought all day
Pent up hurt and anger
The dam breaks
No one can see or hear my cries
My emotional burst
They do not understand
All I hold inside

I can't explain
So please don't ask
I wish I knew how
But, alas I can't
This faceless demon
Holds on tight
Gripping my heart
Squeezing it tight

The void of emptiness
The loneliness and unanswered questions
Eat at my mind
Driving me crazy
Stop the madness
Help me move on
I beseech you
Please help me make it through another night

The new day still grim
Seems a little more manageable
Thank you my dear friend
For holding my hand
Seeing me through another dark night
I know in time
My heart will heal
Until then at least I know
I have you as my friend

Julie Mishler

Raging Tears

Raging storms in the heat of the night
Wind crashing against the windows
Lightning rips across the sky
Rain pours down
As a lone tear silently rolls down the cheek
Of a broken hearted woman
Praying for answers
Searching for hope
Asking why
Why can't he just see me for me
Love me for who I am
Understand what it is I really need

Time slowly passes
The storm rages on
Tears flow freely
Like the rain pouring down
Silently so no one hears
Or sees her pain
The secrets she hides
Deep inside
The unhappiness she feels
Thunder rumbles, shaking the house
Shaking her to the core

Remnants of the storm
Are all that remain
Low and grumbling
She grips her pillow tighter
Her tears subside
Like the earth has been washed clean
So has her soul

This storm is over
She survived once again
The strength and perseverance that she once felt
Sparks a fire within her
Giving her reason to
Weather another storm
Fight another battle
Live to be the woman
She desperately wants to be

Myself

I always wanted
To make you proud
Shine bright
So you could show me off
With your head high
Be a priceless accessory
To have on your arm
Blush when you said
That girl is mine

The time is here
For me to shine
Yet you are gone
So I celebrate alone
These tears of joy
For a job well done
You will never know
Because you are not here
You walked away
Without even so much as a
Goodbye!

You could not see
The good in me
Did not see the potential
Of all I could be
You saw a broken
Tired and battered soul
Down at the bottom
Struggling to get up

You pretended to lift me up
Made me feel
Like I was special
When it suited you
Fit into your game
Then turned around and stomped me down
Leaving me a shell of the woman
I once was

I can promise you this
As I spread my wings
Set my sights on flying
You crippled me
By breaking my wing
You did not kill me
You did not win
I will never give up
You made me fight harder
To prove you wrong
To find myself

If I must stand alone
Celebrate myself
Be proud of myself
Pat myself on my own back
Then I will

I would rather be alone
Then with a man
Who ran away
When the going got tough

Julie Mühler

Call On Me

A million miles away
From where I need you to be
I need you here with me
To slay the dragons
My knight
To reach for my hand
And pull me back up from my plight

The loneliness has crept its way in
The demon of doubt
Dancing about
Laughing as if
You are dressed as a jester
Entertaining his court

Your head hung down
A tear in your eye
You want to fight back
Hold your head high
Stop the incessant laughter
Crush the power they hold over you

Alas you are broken
No fight left
Your mind is weak
Your body fatigued
You lay in a ball
And pray
Pray for the morning light

The dawn of new day
A whisper of hope
The kind words from
A new friend
Warm the heart
Still the pain
Pulls you up
Beckoning you to step forward

Walk with me
Open your eyes
See what is around you
All the little things
Smell the air
Fresh and energizing
Breathe in deep
Take my hand
Walk with me

I promise you this
I will never let go
As long as you need me
My hand is yours to hold
Call on me
For I am here
Reach for me
Say my name
No more will you be alone
Your heart has found a home

Battling An Aching Heart

One of the hardest battles to face in life
Is moving on
Saying goodbye
Letting go
Of a piece of your heart
Not spending every second
Of every day
Thinking about
Wishing for
Hoping still
For what might have been

A day will come
When your heart will not hurt
Just hearing his name
Hearing that song on the radio
You know the one
The one he said reminded him of you
Will not bring tears to your eyes
Maybe you will even sing along

Time will fade the hurt
But no amount of time
Will ever make you forget
All the laughs
The memories
The person you thought you knew
The friend that helped you
Deal with so many things
Made you realize
You could be so much more
Then what you have allowed

What once was clear
Is dark once more
The path is littered
With thorns and weeds
A wall has been erected
You are standing still
Looking for the light
Grasping for hope
To carry you through
Back to the other side

There is always a glimmer of hope
There is always a light
All you have to do is have faith
In the person you are
Who you want to be
Learn from the past
The lessons it taught
Stop beating yourself up
What was cannot be changed
Tear down that wall
Clear the debris
Light those thorns on fire
Seek refuge in what you know is true

You deserve to be happy
You deserve to be loved
You deserve to live
Love yourself
Always be strong

About The Author

Julie Mishler resides in Pennsylvania with her family. When she is not spending time with family, she enjoys writing, reading various genres, art and listening to music.

You can find her on Facebook at:
https://www.facebook.com/authorjuliemishler

Made in the USA
Middletown, DE
11 May 2015